MW00883535

CHRISTIANS
COMMIT SUICIDE

by
Dr. Ronnie W. Goines

KOINONIA CHRISTIAN PUBLISHING

TABLE OF CONTENTS

Preface

I have a confession to make ... I was actually growing more and more slothful in writing this book because I started feeling that there may not be a wide enough interest. Then out of the blue, I found out that another senior pastor committed suicide.

My heart sank because from looking at his social media page or listening to his sermons, suicide would be the last thing one would suspect. Not only is suicide no respecter of person, but it doesn't respect your confession of faith either.

That spirit couldn't care less that we are Christians. In fact, I feel it's a bigger trophy for the enemy when a Christian commits suicide. You see, the enemy, Satan, knows that it can't kill God. It tried that before with Jesus Christ and it didn't work out so well!

So, the next best thing to killing God

is to cause what God loves the most to kill themselves.

People commit suicide for all sorts of reasons. Some even do it as a way punishing or hurting others. What the believer doesn't consider, is how it grieves the heart of God.

Remember how the Bible notes that "Jesus wept" upon seeing where they laid his recently passed friend, Lazarus?

As a pastor, I've seen no greater pain than a parent having to bury a child. The scream that my mother released upon finding out that my sister passed away, still haunts me to this day. 1 John 4:4, as well as other passages throughout the Bible, refer to us as God's "children".

What good parent wouldn't be grieved by a child dying, let alone murdering themselves?

For those reading this that have lost a

loved one to suicide and heard that suicide is a first-class ticket to hell, let me explain how that is bad theology. As our great high priest, the Lord Jesus Christ is constantly interceding on our behalf.

At times when we are not faithful, and the enemy gets the best of us, it does not result in our great high priest ceasing to intercede for us. Even when we are unfaithful, he remains faithful. Yes, we are directed to confess our sins and ask for forgiveness.

So, the question is posited, "How can you ask for forgiveness after you have killed yourself?" The answer is simple.

Our eternal security is based on our initial repentance from sin, not our ongoing confession of sin. The directive in James 5:16 to 'confess our sins' refers to how a healthy body of believers are to interact. It was not a mandate making it necessary to confess a sin to God.

Why? Because he already knows.

God knew that Adam had sinned before he confessed what had happened. The reason we acknowledge our sins while in prayer is because it displays humility and dependence on him. This usually leads to him removing the guilt from that particular sin, but salvation was never at jeopardy.

The atoning blood of Jesus Christ is not washed away by the gravest mistakes.

1
The Good Shepherd

Psalm 23 is composed of 6 verses that have become the hallmark of assurance as it pertains to the good shepherd being responsible for the provision and protection of the sheep under his care. Verses 1-2 both deal with basic physical needs like rest, food, and water. You know, what can be seen.

But the remaining 4 verses add other things to the good shepherd's job description. Things that impact sheep that can't be seen. Things like peace of mind, conduct, fear, companionship, happiness, and security!

Did you know that the things that can't be seen are often much deadlier than what can be seen? I read a book earlier this year by Phillip Keller. In it, he wrote about a season shepherds refer to as "fly time".

Fly time is a reference to the hordes of insects that emerge with the advent of warm weather. Those who have kept livestock or studied wildlife are well aware of the serious problems presented by insects in the summer.

Many of the parasites that trouble the flock and make their lives miserable are warble flies, bot flies, heel flies, nasal flies, deer flies, black flies, mosquitoes, gnats, and several other small winged parasites that proliferate at this time of year. Their attacks can readily turn warm summer months into a time of torture.

One of the flies serving as the greatest nuisance to the flock are nasal flies. These flies buzz about the sheep's head, attempting to deposit their eggs on the damp mucous membranes of the sheep's nose. If they are successful, the eggs will hatch in a few days to form small, slender, worm-like larvae.

They work their way up the nasal passages into the sheep's head, burrowing into their flesh. This creates an intense irritation accompanied by severe inflammation. Attempting to get relief, sheep will deliberately beat their heads against trees, rocks, posts, or brush.

Can you imagine what these sheep look like behaving like this! It looks as though they're attempting to kill themselves? When in reality, they're seeking relief from what going on in their heads!

In some cases, sheep will panic and run until they drop from sheer exhaustion. Why? Because you and I both know you can't outrun your mind. Ewes that suffer from this condition start losing weight to the point where they stop milking their young. Don't miss that! Not only does the adult ewe suffer, but her babies too.

Can you imagine these sheep being so internally bothered that they stop providing for their babies? It's not that they don't want to be good parents. It's that they have things happening in their head!

Now if you're watching this with a shepherd's loving eyes, you know EXACTLY what's going on. You know that if a usually calm, docile, amicable sheep starts acting like a raving mad dog, then there must be something going on in its head! Not it's heart, but it's head!

This is very important because individuals who entertain suicide may have the sweetest of hearts, but the enemy has gotten into their heads.

For the Christian contemplating suicide, it is important that you realize you are going through a type of spiritual fly time. The destructive lifestyle choices or attempts to harm yourself are the result of unclean spirits that have gained access to your mind.

But there is good news! The good shepherd knows exactly what is going on.

So the question is, "what do I do when my mind starts slipping in the wrong direction"? "What do I do when my heart is committed, but my mind is not faithful?" "What do I do when my heart is at peace with Jesus, but my mind is at war with everyone and everything, including me?"

What about when my heart is telling me "Don't do it!", but my mind is constantly whispering "Do it! Why not?"

THE REMEDY

At the very first sign of fly time among the flock, the shepherd will apply an anecdotal ointment to their heads. The ingredients of sulfur, spices, and olive oil are all mixed together and then smeared over the nose and head of the sheep. This ointment will not only serve as protection against nasal flies, but it kills the ones that are already there.

Furthermore, once the oil has been applied to the sheep's head, there is an immediate change in behavior. Gone is the aggravation. Gone is the frenzy and panic. Gone is the irritability and restlessness. Instead, the sheep will start to feed quietly again. Then soon lie down to get some much-needed rest.

In a similar way, since we are engaged in daily spiritual warfare there are times that the evil one gets into our heads. It is nothing new and not a sign of weakness! Many bible characters at one time or another found themselves with "flies in their heads".

- Adam rationalized in his mind that he'd be ok eating what was forbidden because it was coming from someone he trusted.

- Ananias and Sapphira thought it better to lie than be honest.

- Both Sarah and Zechariah reasoned that certain things were just too hard for God.

- And of course, Job's wife, Elijah, and Jonah all mentally concluded that dying would be better than living!

These mental nuisances don't just stop with our thoughts. They begin to affect and even change our behavior leading us to do or act in a manner that is so out of character that we not only stop looking like ourselves; but will eventually disgrace ourselves and the Jesus we say we serve.

The reason we need to take thoughts

captive when they present themselves as adversarial to the Lord is because they are the seeds to a sinful action.

The ointment that our Good Shepherd has provided us to both prevent and destroy unwanted thoughts are prayer, fellowship, accountability, serving, and the Word of God!

Like the suffering sheep during fly time, we are to be fully immersed in the ointment that's produced by combining these four ingredients.

Be sure to understand! The ointments applied to the ailing sheep's head are only temporary and may only last for a few hours. Before you get discouraged by thinking the whole process of smearing ointment was a waste of time, here is a good place to tell you that the Good Shepherd will continuously apply this ointment in order to keep his flock free from these types of nasty parasites.

What's even better is that He has

plenty of ointment!

Listen, it only takes one confession of faith to be saved. One faith. One baptism. But when it comes to the covering of your mind, it's a continual thing.

Let there be no doubt about it, where as your salvation is eternal, the ointment that protects the mind from evil thoughts is to be an intentional and perpetual effort.

2
Suicide's a BULLY!

The thoughts, which are inaudible, yet deafening voices, just won't stop. They persist like a bully that has no idea when enough is enough! It is overwhelming, and I fear there is nothing left to do. The thoughts, the voices, how can I make them stop? This is all my fault.

How could it have gotten so difficult? No one sees me slowly dying inside. No one notices the pain that I suffer from. No one is there for me. They tell me to pray, but is God even listening?

I've prayed and yet they still linger! What is there left for me to do other than to find a way to make it stop permanently. I am trying to bear my cross, but this burden is just too heavy. I can't carry this anymore. These thoughts, the voices they continue to tell me I am worthless. I am nothing.

No one loves me. No one cares about me. I am defeated. There is no one I can trust. Everyone is against me. It's all my fault. I do not see the good in any of it. I am tired and just want it all to end.

Do any of the aforementioned declarations sound familiar? I wish I could tell you that Christians don't ever have any of these thoughts mentioned above, but that would be a lie.

As a Pastor, I've had many individuals confess to me that they struggle with increased depression and stress. Suicide seems to be the most reasonable resolve!

The gateway for these demonic whispers manifest through a plethora of situations spanning from broken relationships, extended financial crisis, guilt due to a mistake that hurt someone they love, or sometimes the fatigue of dealing with a medical condition. The prolonged stress and difficulty coping with life circumstances leads to chronic depression.

In this book, we'll look at individuals like Jonah, who despite knowing God, had a series of bouts with depression, anger, and bitterness that led him to embrace thoughts of suicide. His depression wasn't the result of relationship, financial, or medical issues. His desire to quit on life was triggered by him not wanting to do what God told him to do.

Attempting to flee from the call that God has on your life, ultimately leads to death. After Jonah's first recorded bout with suicide he noted

"To the roots of the mountains I sank down; the earth beneath barred me in forever. But you, LORD my God, brought my life up from the pit" (Jonah 2:6).

Jonah is thanking God for sparing him from what he was convinced that

DR. RONNIE W. GOINES

he wanted: TO DIE.   All is well in Jonah's mind. But not long after … the torment   begins   again.

3
So, you think you can RUN?

Jonah received a word from the Lord to preach to the city of Nineveh for their sin against God. Instead, Jonah chose to flee to the city of Tarshish away from God's presence. Sometimes what God calls us to do does not align with what we want to do. When our plan is not his plan, great discomfort arises.

Anytime that we attempt to flee God's presence, marks the beginning of frustration, anger, bitterness, and depression. This happened quickly with Jonah. When a storm came, he volunteered the ship's crew to throw him into the sea.

So, in a real sense, Jonah chose suicide by sea. What is interesting is upon them throwing him into the sea, he began to pray for God to save him.

In today's society, we see Christians attempting to distance themselves from God when they have trying times in their lives. Suicide affects everyone. Those who entertain the very thought of the action, have little intention of going through with it. But as life continues to throw blows that shake someone from the foundation up, suicide becomes more appealing.

Failed relationships, grief, financial distress, medical issues, and lack of success can lead to severe depression. In fact, a loss of any type is a major risk factor.

It is completely natural and normal to have bad and discouraging days sometimes, but if that low mood remains day after day, it could indicate depression. Depression is a very common mood disorder that has an outstanding effect on how you think, feel, and handle daily activities.

This mental illness does not signify weakness or a negative personality, however, its severity interrupts one's ability to see the good in anything.

Major Depressive Disorder is diagnosed after one experiences depressive symptoms for more than two weeks. Severe and chronic stress and related events typically lead to depression. A depressed mood is usually identified by feeling sad, down, empty, irritable, cranky, loss of interest in enjoyable activities, insomnia, fatigue, feelings of worthlessness, and recurrent thoughts of death or suicidal ideas.

Many people suffering from depression, can't express why they feel the way they feel. The disease can trick you into believing that there is no purpose or call on your life. The fear of inadequacy and failure proffers consequential psychological threats to self-motivation.

It's hard for someone who is depressed to recognize that what they are feeling is abnormal, which is why untreated depression often leads to suicide.

Consequently, suicide in itself is a taboo topic. Culturally, no one wants to talk or even think about it. It's uncomfortable. Suicidal people don't want to feel as if they are burdening others with their problems. Some feel unworthy of help. Others simply do not know where to start or what to say. They believe that if someone cared, they would notice their change in demeanor.

Individuals battling suicidal thoughts have rationalized that others don't and won't understand, so why bother. For this reason, many will keep it to themselves. Families of those who attempt and complete suicide are usually blindsided by the act.

Suicide for many friends and families

is like a thief in the night. It takes the most precious possession from you without warning. Loved ones often question why and how they missed the signs. They wonder what could have been so bad. Society looks at suicidal individuals as weak minded, failures, those that give up and in too easily.

But society doesn't realize how long that person was fighting for their life, wrestling and struggling with the very desire to harm themselves.

I will never forget when a childhood friend put a .45 caliber gun to his head and pulled the trigger. Later that night as we gathered to mourn, one of my friends made the statement, "I can't believe he was that weak!" But none of us realized until reading the letter that he left, how long he struggled in his mind.

Not only was he having nightmares from multiple murders he witnessed; he also battled HIV. What's profound is that several months prior, he accepted Christ!

It is not our innate nature to want to die. We were designed to survive. But the ambivalence of someone experiencing severe depression weighs heavy on them daily. Even Jonah when coming face to face with death, cried out to God to save him with praises of thanksgiving.

To illustrate, think about what it's like being on the swing set. You constantly go back and forth, until you reach the peak. Once you've reached the top, you have to decide whether you are going to ground yourself or jump off. Depressed people suffering from suicidal ideations, battle this every day.

Until they feel they can't fight anymore and jump! They are tired of swinging and they no longer have the patience to wait until the swing lacks the inertia to stop on its own and ground them again.

Furthermore, suicide reminds me of an abuser in a domestic violence relationship. Preying on the frail and most vulnerable. And even those that we perceive to have it all together, such as the wealthy, successful, and famed; get caught up in the manipulative trap.

The aggressor in violent relationships seeks to isolate, withdraw, and destroy their partner. They beat you down mentally, physically, and emotionally until you fall dependent upon them. And to keep you in their grasp, they give you momentary, temporary breaks from the torture. Until it is time to cycle the abuse again.

Suicide is the exact same way. It plays on the blame and guilt you feel for situations and circumstances you are in. It is relentless in its attempt to destroy you. It plays on your psyche so much, that it is hard to separate the emotion from the logic.

The ultimate goal of the spirit of suicide is to take you outside of God's presence, so that it can lead you down a destructive path.

And it starts off small, typically with feelings of loneliness, mood swings, hopelessness, overwhelming stress, overbearing sadness, and inability to sleep.

So, we try to mask the pain or use indirect methods to self-harm. For example, you will see many adolescents begin to cut. They will try to cover their arms and legs more often than usual, so their behavior goes unnoticed. Small children often draw disturbing pictures or act out significantly from the norm at home or at school.

This often goes ignored and misdiagnosed for ADHD, when in fact it is depression. Many teenagers and adults begin to use and abuse drugs and alcohol, join gangs, or participate in risky sexual activity. Others simply engage in high risk hobbies that could lead to death.

Some of these people are often labeled as "Adrenalin Junkies". Individuals suffering from chronic illnesses may stop going to treatment or quit taking their medications.

These dangerous lifestyle choices can lead to one's demise and often do. Once a person begins to indulge in behaviors that are detrimental to their growth and relationship with Christ, demonic attacks have their gateway to come through.

Depression fosters the desperation and the constant whisper to not only thinking about killing oneself but developing a plan to put the thought into action.

4

Are you Angry with God … For real?

Suicide is a form of anger against oneself with the intention to harm in the most final way. In Jonah's second contemplation of suicidal ideation, he found himself angry with God.

In Jonah 4:2-3 he prayed to the Lord, "O Lord, is this not what I said when I was in my country? That is why I tried to flee to Tarshish; for I know you are a gracious God and merciful, slow to anger, and abounding in steadfast love, and relenting from disaster. Therefore now, O Lord, please take my life from me, for it is better for me to die than to live."

And God with almost a joking tenor asked Jonah, "Are you seriously angry right now?"

Before you judge Jonah too harshly, let me tell you that nothing can throw you back to a state of depression and anger faster than feeling that God has let you down. Whenever a person feels that they can't depend on God they're in a really bad place. This can foster hopelessness.

Once an individual feels hopeless, suicide begins to whisper. "You're nothing, nobody loves you, not even your God!" "There is only one way to stop feeling this way… end it! Take your life! No one will miss you, no one will care. Everyone is better off without you here!"

Most people suffering with depression express it through anger versus sadness. A primary emotion of fear, sadness, and anxiety can feel uncomfortable to reveal because of social stigma. In turn, we often transform the true emotion we are feeling into anger, which is more socially acceptable.

Anger does not come off as a "weak" emotion. Depression masked as anger and aggression is usually seen in children, men, and adolescents. Which can help to explain why many friends and family are unaware that they are suffering from a deep sadness. It is perceived instead, that they have an anger issue.

Anger is an emotional reaction to pain, hopelessness, and frustration. Anger can be a motivator or cycle in feelings of rage and defeat. Depressed individuals turn this anger inward. Due to the intensity of the pain, angry people typically lash out at others, and when they notice the effect it causes everyone else, they completely isolate themselves and become withdrawn.

Jonah left the city of Nineveh and went to sit by himself towards the east. Isolation is where despair becomes very dangerous and suicidal thoughts begin to take place.

When someone reaches a point that they can no longer find happiness, comfort, and relief from their suffering; suicide becomes more opportune. Depressed people have difficulty seeing life optimistically. Even Christians who endure this mental illness, know that joy comes in the morning, but struggle in believing that in their current season.

Suicide plays on that hopelessness and the torment eventually leads to death. Jonah saw death as an end to a means of what is seeming as unbearable heartache and pain.

Suicide's influence grows with every situation that increases the hurt, pain, shame, and guilt that depressed individuals feel. Despite Jonah's disposition towards God, God was still concerned about Jonah.

The text says that while Jonah was in the heat and could have suffered from heat exhaustion or a heat stroke; God provided shade for him. Isn't that just like God, that even when we pout, he still provides!

It is completely understandable that Jonah was thankful for God's provision. However, he made the mistake that many of us often make today. He took more comfort in what God provided than he did in the provider.

We know this because when the plant that provided the shade was removed, guess what Jonah declares in Chapter 4:8; "It is better for me to die, than to live." So God once again with an almost comical tenor asks, "So you mad about the plant?" Jonah digs his heels in and replies to the Lord, "Yes I'm mad, I have had enough! I should die." He found himself angry with God, again. This was Jonah's final bout with suicide.

It's dangerous to place more value in what God gives than God Himself. Be it marriage, assets, position of influence, or careers; never place the provision above the Provider. Sometimes, God removes provision in order to show us where He REALLY stands with us.

Think about it! If your joy, confidence, and peace of mind were all rooted in God, then you will feel secure in knowing they remain, even when material things are lost. God is still there.

For instance, if I built a six-story house of cards on an immaculate dinner table, and the house of cards fell down, my joy is still intact because of the table in which it was constructed still stands. It's all about perspective. In case you missed that, God is the immaculate dinner table and anything that He ever blesses us to be stewards over, are just cards.

Jonah, like many suicidal people, reached his limit. Each time he thought he reached a point of rest or championed a challenge, another arose. Jonah felt he couldn't catch a break. The final contemplation of suicide occurred after his momentary relief withered away.

Dealing with the loss of a temporary convenience that was thought to last a lifetime, is discouraging for a person suffering from depression. That's why it's so important to take care of ourselves and heal following a divorce. It doesn't matter if the marriage was a fairy tale or a nightmare.

Divorce is still hard! Because the hurt of losing the one person you were supposed to do life with forever, can send you into a whirl wind of anger, bitterness, loneliness, and sadness.

When you're depressed, you often lack the ability to separate the logic from the emotion. Your body is in a constant stress related state. Depression places people in a severe emotional turmoil and rather than utilizing the fight or flight response, those suffering often turn to suicide.

The fight or flight response is a physiological reaction to mental or physical stress. The response prepares the body to stay and deal with, fight the stressor, or flee it. Fight or flight is important because it is our instinctive mechanism for survival.

When in fight or flight, our cognitive (neocortex) and emotional (mammalian) brain shut off and our reptilian (survival) brain activates. Its function regulates the homeostasis of the body. When depressed, the brain is unable to differentiate what circumstances are significant stressors.

Suicidal individuals are under so much stress that their body is in a constant fight or flight, and they no longer want to fight or escape. They just want it all to end. They choose suicide because the glimpse of hope for safety and security is fleeting. Those electing to take their own lives no longer have the ability to rationalize or find ways to adapt to their present circumstances. They break down.

Naturally, people are resilient and able to process and move forward from difficult and stressful life events. However, when our stress levels become chronic it leads to major depression.

Both positive and negative experiences can contribute to a significant stressor that prompt depressive symptoms. There are three different intensity levels of stress: eustress, distress, and dysfunction.

Eustress

Eustress is a motivating stressor. It's like going after a degree. Exams, papers, class discussions, group projects and reading text books may stress you throughout the process. But you are determined to complete the degree to push you to the next level.

Those events may have stressed you out, but they also drove you to work harder and level up. We see this with the apostle Paul and James.

Paul writes in Philippians 3:13-14 that despite all the trials he's had to endure he's going to "press on towards the mark"! In other words, the mark he's striving for is worth the stress he's enduring to attain it.

This is why he's able to command Timothy, in 2 Timothy 2:3, to "endure hardship as a good soldier of Jesus Christ"! In James 1:2-3, James instructs us to "count it all joy" during stressful seasons because we'll be better and stronger afterwards.

Christians are NOT exempt from

stress. In fact, God sometimes uses it to stretch us in our maturation.

Distress

Distress is caused by excessive stressors, however, the majority of people exhibit resilience at this level of intensity. Distress can be found in multiple forms. It can cause problems with the way you think, feel, behave or act, and can even impact your spirituality. Like when a family member dies in a car accident.

One may endure an inability to concentrate or make decisions, anxiety, irritability, mood swings, fear, grief, impulsivity, alcohol or drug use, and family discord. Spiritually, like Jonah, we may exhibit anger with God and question his sovereignty.

It's common to withdraw ourselves from our church or community of believers that we do life with. We also may question our own faith. But eventually we find it in our being to overcome the obstacle and continue to move forward in life.

In 2 Samuel 12:26-23 we find a gripping account of David dealing with the loss of a child. As would any parent, he found himself under deep distress. The text reports that not only did he not eat, but he laid on the ground all night while his child was sick.

When the child finally died, David's servants feared telling David for fear that he'd commit suicide (2 Samuel 12:18)! Yet, David shows why he's been dubbed as a man after God's own heart.

How? Because upon learning that the child had passed, David arose from the ground, dusted himself off, bathed, changed clothes, went to the temple to worship the Lord, and then went home to eat!

His servants were absolutely dumbfounded at how he went from such a deep state of mourning, to a place of worship. Here's how David responded to their inquiry, He said, "While the child was still alive, I fasted and wept, for I said, 'Who knows whether the Lord will be gracious to me that the child may live?' 23 But now he is dead.

Why should I fast? Can I bring him back again? I shall go to him, but he will not return to me." Wow! I'm not honestly not sure I'd be able to bounce back as quickly as David if anything were to happen to one of my children.

But I take console in him laying out a model to strive for if I needed it. David never put God on trial for the sickness or death of his child.

He trusted and believed wholeheartedly that God would heal his child, but when God's will was shown in contrary David continued to worship Him! David's faith in God was firm and unshakeable.

He knew that the only way to face this giant loss was how he faced a giant once before by the name of Goliath... by faith."

Dysfunction

Dysfunction, on the other hand, is where depression and suicide sets in. This stress level impairs the ability to complete normal, day to day activities and leaves you unable to take care of your responsibilities. Similar to the adult ewe suffering from fly time.

Dysfunction causes persistent hopelessness and helplessness, suicidal and homicidal ideations, disabling guilt, and diminished problem solving. Emotionally it can create panic attacks, child-like emotional outbursts, depression, avoidance, and numbing of emotions.

Behaviorally, it leads to violence, abuse of others, self-medication, and decreases in personal hygiene. Dysfunction also prompts physical symptoms of chest pain, recurrent dizziness, irregular heartbeats, and frequent headaches, to name a few. Severe spiritual dysfunction can lead to the cessation of practicing your faith and religious hallucinations or delusions.

A biblical case study would be Saul. In 1 Samuel 10:22, he was so stressed and afraid about being chosen as the first king that he hid. In his final days, Saul was tormented with hallucinations and violent outbursts. (I guess some promotions just aren't worth it.)

Not only do we see in 1 Samuel 18:11-12 how Saul's distress prompted him to attempt to murder David while in a jealous rage, but later in I Samuel 20:33 we see that he also threw a spear at his own son, Johnathan! When a person is under extreme distress they're not only a danger to themselves, but to those around them!

Of course, the classic case of dysfunction that ended in suicide would be Judas, who as we read in Matthew 27:1-10, was so inundated with guilt after betraying Jesus that he hung himself."

Depression can be overbearing, and temporary happiness may feel like a breath of fresh air. A small glimpse of hope keeps suicide at bay. Hope also derails suicidal ideations from turning into suicide attempts. Minor wins, people showing interest or care, a break from the thoughts or voices can serve as temporary relief from severe depression.

The word of God admonishes us to not forsake the assembly. In other words, it illuminates why we should all have a good church home. Church is a place where people show interest and that they care. A place where you matter.

I once had a member who was overtaken by deep depression when she left our church and no longer served in a ministry. She called me and was in a drunken stupor. She railed about losing the only break from her life that she had. Koinonia Christian Church was her place of belonging and significance.

Serving the Lord despite her circumstances aided in keeping her depression from consuming her. Outside of that, she was lost and felt alone.

5
Suicide's Modus Operandi

Suicide is the act of taking one's own life. An attempt of suicide is typically in response to overwhelming and unbearable emotional pain. Most people have thoughts about suicide at least once in their life. There is active and passive suicidal ideation (SI).

Those experiencing active SI, have an intense desire to die and formulate a plan to carry out their death. Passive SI, on the other hand, involves a desire to die without a specific plan.

Suicidal people usually do not ask for help. That doesn't mean that the help is not needed or warranted. People suffering with SI, do not want to die, they just want to relieve the pain. To prevent suicide, we all must be aware of the warning signs and take action.

The spirit of suicide attempts to

convince you that how you are feeling right now is how you will always feel. It tries to ensure that making a permanent decision is the only way to end temporary emotion or is the only resolve to a temporary problem.

Depression can be a chronic illness which is why it is important to learn to manage it in appropriate and healthy ways.

For this reason, the suicidal spirit operates on impulse. Impulsivity is one of suicides greatest allies. This is because impulsive behaviors happen without any rational thought or logic. Suicidal thoughts makes one feel as if they have no other choice, they have no power.

It banks on the belief that you either have no idea of how much God loves you, or your present hurt has made you forget his love for you.

But suicide is the most preventable death! Every problem has a solution and every circumstance only lasts for a season. At its core, suicide calls God a liar, redefines who God says you are, and goes against scripture. This justifies the necessity to not just memorize scripture, but to believe and walk in it daily.

Here are a few of my favorites that I encourage every believer to memorize:

Psalms 30:5 "For his anger is but for a moment, and his favor is for a lifetime. Weeping may tarry for the night, but joy comes with the morning."

Psalms 2:2-6 "The kings of the earth set themselves, and the rulers take counsel together, against the Lord and against his Anointed, saying, 'Let us burst their bonds apart   and cast away their cords from us.'

He who sits in the heavens laughs; the Lord holds them in derision. Then he will speak to them in his wrath, and terrify them in his fury, saying, "As for me, I have set my King on Zion, my holy hill."

Psalms 37:23-24 "The steps of a man are established by the Lord, when he delights in his way; though he fall, he shall not be cast headlong, for the Lord upholds his hand.

Psalms 37:25 "I have been young, and now am old, yet I have not seen the righteous forsaken or his children begging for bread.

2 Corinthians 4:8-9, 17, 18 "We are afflicted in every way, but not crushed; perplexed, but not driven to despair; persecuted, but not forsaken; struck down, but not destroyed; …

For this light momentary affliction is preparing for us an eternal weight of glory beyond all comparison, as we look not to the things that are seen but to the things that are unseen. For the things that are seen are transient, but the things that are unseen are eternal."

Colossians 3:1-2 "If then you have been raised with Christ, seek the things that are above, where Christ is, seated at the right hand of God. Set your minds on things that are above, not on things that are on earth."

Romans 8:28 "And we know that for those who love God all things work together for good, for those who are called according to his purpose." This one is my most favorite.

Romans 8:24-25 "For in this hope we were saved. Now hope that is seen is not hope. For who hopes for what he sees? But if we hope for what we do not see, we wait for it with patience."

Romans 15:13 "May the God of hope fill you with all joy and peace in believing, so that by the power of the Holy Spirit you may abound in hope."

Philippians 3:13-14: "Brothers, I do not consider that I have made it my own. But one thing I do: forgetting what lies behind and straining forward to what lies ahead, I press on toward the goal for the prize of the upward call of God in Christ Jesus."

Philippians 1:6 "And I am sure of this, that he who began a good work in you will bring it to completion at the day of Jesus Christ."

1 Peter 5:10 "And after you have suffered a little while, the God of all grace, who has called you to his eternal glory in Christ, will himself restore, confirm, strengthen, and establish you."

Joshua 10:25 "And Joshua said to them, "Do not be afraid or dismayed; be strong and courageous. For thus the Lord will do to all your enemies against whom you fight."

Jeremiah 29:11 "For I know the plans I have for you, declares the Lord, plans for welfare[a] and not for evil, to give you a future and a hope."

Isaiah 40:31 "but they who wait for the Lord shall renew their strength; they shall mount up with wings like eagles; they shall run and not be weary; they shall walk and not faint.

I would suggest that you read these every morning before starting your day. They will come in handy when you enter a season where you need encouragement.

Suicide influences people of all ages and in every stage of life. Statistics show that suicide is the tenth leading cause of death in the United States. That equates to about 44,000 Americans every year. For every completed suicide, there were 25 attempts.

And although women are more likely to attempt suicide, men are more likely to complete it.

Women attempt suicide twice as many times as men. However, men are actually successful twice as much. Well there's a reason for this. You see our culture is conducive for making it easier for men to exude suicidal tendencies undetected.

Allow me to show how a suicidal precursor is embraced when exhibited by a man but would be noted as odd if the same is seen by a woman.

Let's start with how depressed individuals sometimes desire to cut communication off from everyone. Most would deem it unusual for a wife to lock herself away in a room and not communicate with her husband or children for hours at a time, which typically signifies that there is something wrong.

On the contrary, men isolate themselves in their "man caves" and it indicates "strength" in their silence. Rather than, an unaddressed emotional issue.

If a woman got drunk every weekend,

she'd almost immediately be seen as a candidate for AA. However, this same habit for men tailgating, or at bars watching sporting events, is seen as normative.

What about promiscuity? I don't have to tell you what's said about women who have multiple sex partners, not to mention those who have sex with multiple men at the same time! But a man with multiple sex partners is a "player", ladies' man", or "boys will be boys".

A man who sleeps with more than one woman at once is deemed a "ROCK STAR"! Even violence towards others is weighed on a different scale. If two women fight each other it's deemed as "unladylike ", but if two men fight, it's called "settling it as men"!

The unclean spirit of suicide figures if it can skew how man's "help meet" sees him, it'll be easier to kill him. This is huge because when many men commit suicide it's commonly associated with woman hurt. You typically see these as crimes of passion, fatal attractions, and murder-suicides.

The enemy wants to disfigure and skew the image of a man to a woman. When a wife loses hope for her husband, she's less apt to be a help meet. Why? Because it's hard to garner the energy to help what has no hope.

It's for this reason men and those around them have to be especially aware of depression and suicidal indicators. It's my opinion, the reason men are actually more successful in their suicide attempts than women, is because they are able to suffer emotionally undetected for longer lengths of time.

On top of the fact, that men are naturally more likely to take aggressive and lethal means with their attempts at suicide. For instance, using guns or other weapons instead of taking pills.

The enemy has a similar ploy with attempting to skew man's paradigm toward women. Woman was/is God's precious gift to man. The woman was so precious in God's eye that he didn't even create her until testing Adam. It was only after Adam cut the grass trimmed the shrubs and become familiar with the animals by naming them did God bless him Eve!

In other words, God had no intention of blessing Adam with a woman without a track record of responsibility. Adam loved and cherished Eve. Even after she made a mistake Adam honored her. How? Adam could've easily named her according to her folly: Snake Whisperer, Naïve, Nerd, Sinner.

But instead he called her Eve, source of all living.

Today, Satan has tirelessly attacked this first image of woman held by man.

Now, it's common for a woman to work to take care of a man. Instead of being seen as the source of all living, culture has painted them as mere sex objects.

I can go on and on about the stress levels of women living in a society fueled by narcissism and misogyny. 100 years ago, being a single mother was like wearing a 'scarlet letter' of shame. Today, being a single mother has become culturally acceptable because many men, while ok with a 'baby mama', are afraid of committing to a wife.

At least 65% of all women are victims of some form of sexual misconduct or sexual assault by age 16! Because of a deep distrust for men, some women would rather have another woman as their mate as opposed to risking being hurt by a man.

There's so much more to be said about the devil's tactics to destroy how men and women see each other, but you get my point.

As stated earlier, when we are outside of the presence of God, angry or emotionally withdrawn from God, and depending on temporary sources for our joy, it is easy for the spirit of suicide and other attacks of the enemy to take place.

Research shows that there are several other factors that makes individuals at an increased risk for suicidal ideations. These include family history of suicidal thoughts or attempts, depression, bipolar disorder, or other disorders; experiencing significant childhood traumas; loss (relational, social, work, or financial); and alcohol and substance abuse.

There are four different categories of symptoms that can be noticed when a person is heading down a suicidal path. These include **behavioral**, **physical**, **cognitive**, and **psychosocial** symptoms. Behavioral symptoms have been discussed frequently throughout this book.

Some examples are isolating and stating "I'm just tired … I wish I could fall asleep and never wake up!" Many people give away prized possessions, withdraw from things they enjoy, become extremely impulsive, and increase risky lifestyle behaviors.

Physical warning signs include scars or injuries from past attempts and changes in eating habits or sleeping habits. For example, you or your loved one may have difficulty falling asleep, staying asleep, or unable to get out of bed in the morning.

Cognitive symptoms may be a little more difficult to recognize. This is because most suicidal people are not openly expressive. Especially about the belief that dying by suicide is the only way to end their emotional pain. They may, however, seem to have a preoccupation with death and dying. Constantly researching death, watching videos, or talking about it.

Psychosocial symptoms deal mostly in the emotional realm of the suicidal process. They include feeling hopeless, helpless, trapped, paranoid, psychotic, and self-loathing. A change you may be able to identify are sudden changes in personality, mood swings, severe anxiety, agitation, and irritability.

It can be extremely dangerous if someone has a significant change from major depressed to extremely happy state. The suicidal person may at that time have the desire, plan, means, and energy to attempt to kill themselves.

It's key to be sure that you don't overlook some of these symptoms. It's easy to discount them as just a moody teenager, or spoiled kid. She's just an introvert or he's just a "hot head".

There is something going on that is deeper than the outwardly expressed emotion.

We have to be more aware and pay a little closer attention. It has to be taken seriously!

Take time to be in tune with your emotions and find positive and healthy ways to cope with your stress. Talk to someone, even if you don't need feedback, just don't let it internalize and bottle up. Do things you enjoy!

Exercise, fish, dance, play sports, watch movies, spend time with friends and family, take a long bath, relax, get a massage, read your bible, go on vacation, or anything else that can help you to unwind and destress.

So, I know you may be questioning, "Pastor, you've said all this to mean what?" "How am I supposed to know what to do?" Simply start by being more aware and take interest past the surface of those you love. Even those you may not know but are around a lot. Begin to notice. Be intentional. Pray for them. Let them know that you are here with them.

Not only is it important to say you are there, but be present, in the moment. Empathize. Don't ask why! Ask how! "How can I help?" "Do you feel safe?" "What do you need?" Let people know that they are valued and remind them of God's love. And when they pretend that nothing is going on., like the suicidal spirit, persist!

Don't give up on them! Continue to question, affirm, and be there for them! You can and will save a life!

6

Notes from a Few that SURVIVED!

A Man under PRESSURE...

Depression? Who knew I would suffer from it. I watched my mom suffer with it all the time, so I felt prepared. In one month, all that changed and I stopped being this energetic, fun, and cool guy to be around. It happened in February.

A month after I got out of the military and just short of a month away from my daughter's birth, I lost myself, and all hope for life. That's when I attempted suicide.

I had been going through the motions for a while before the incident. The mood swings, losing my appearance, drinking heavy, drugs, just living careless and reckless. I kept it hidden from everyone and stayed to myself.

I was alone in the world and felt I had

no one to go to. How I felt about my family was that no one really cared about me. Most of my emotions stem from my breaking point with my family letting me down. None of my accomplishments were good enough for them to be there for me.

Now having my second daughter, I questioned myself because I never really knew how to be there for my first. I just went through a divorce, which took a toll on me I never expected. This too is another reason I found myself to be depressed.

You see! I searched for a lot of things through the women I dated and people I have had in my life. The feeling of being empty hurt me physically. It felt like a constant pounding at my heart.

This cloud of darkness made me numb emotionally and mentally. The idea of killing myself was more convincing every day.

It came to a point that I forgot all about the issues I was going through and focused more on the feelings I was enduring and the voices in my head. It became overwhelming and too powerful to handle. That's when I decided to end the pain.

I went to grab my Glock 40 from my bag. I checked the magazine to make sure it was loaded and had one in the chamber. I walked in my bedroom to my sleeping baby girl and girlfriend. Gave them both kisses. Whispered in their ear "I love you and sorry I couldn't be there".

I took one last shot of Hennessy and sat on the floor in front of my bed. I stared at my daughter and girlfriend, then click, click… Nothing happens, but the movement of my girlfriend standing over me as she kneeled down to wrap her arms around me ever so tightly to where I almost couldn't breathe. She asked nothing, but allowed me to cry in her arms.

As all of this was going on, I couldn't help to ask "how am I still here ... what happened?" It didn't dawn on me that a week prior to this incident, when I dropped my gun, I broke the firing pin which caused the gun to jam when I pulled the trigger.

In that moment of relief, I questioned my purpose for living. In all honesty, I was even more upset that I wasn't dead. Now, I have to face all of this. I couldn't just leave it hidden. I was more confused and yet at peace. That night made one thing clear to me; that life is not in my control.

I would like to encourage the next person who feels empty, alone, like your world is crashing down on you. To seek spiritual help, talk about how you're feeling, don't hold it all in.

That's our biggest mistake. To think we're strong enough to manage and overcome, but we're not. That "empty" feeling is the worst mental state anyone can be in.

The hardest thing to do is talking about to someone because we're embarrassed about it. In reality, you can't do it alone! Don't try and fight the feeling on your own because you will lose that battle.

A Woman Survives Death and Divorce …

I remember it so clearly. It is a still portrait of that moment. The moment when I, seriously and definitively, decided … I was going to end it all.

I was driving to my apartment in jeered silence with recurring thoughts and memories of betrayals by my husband. Already suffering from depression, I had finally made up my mind: "I'm going to kill myself. I'm going to take as many Tylenol pills that I have as soon as I get home."

Times before, I had held several jeweled sedations in my hand—sort of like candy—and had played with their lifeless beauty to grant me a kind of deliverance from the constant torment in head.

I despised the visual remembrance of an unforgiveable mistake of marriage to a man I surmised duped me. I no longer could continue to put on the show for everyone, so I planned my demise.

One thing that definitely mattered to me, was how will I look when I'm dead? I had toyed in mental contemplation for months. Really, the method of escape was important, for it would impact my looks, my presentation. And, surely, my family would dress me, impeccably, and my make-up—oh, it would be flawless, even better than I had ever worn it.

For months, I had envisioned how beautiful I would look, especially since I relished wearing stylish apparel; it was my signature, so it only made sense: "preserve your looks". At least, I had control of that final part of my life.

Then, as quickly as I had determined the best physical preservation of death, one that seemingly offered a gentle and less intrusive appeal that would calm any anxiety, two portraits flashed on my windshield. They were abrupt and paralyzing.

A picture of my brother and my Daddy appeared, like magic, as an intentional last resort. Now, I know it was God's final "hail Mary", since I had ignored all other interruptions of my dreamy, slightly romantic suicide. God had arrested me!

He had enough of this toil with my mind and emotions that the enemy had housed within me. However, I could even see the headline: "Teacher Found Dead—But Why?" And I was reaching my deadline.

It's just hard you know? After losing my Momma, my voice and spiritual surge and support, I spiraled into a mental and psychological depression. To avoid "dealing with grief" of this magnitude, I feverously worked job after job.

Literally, I worked every day from morning to night—and crisscrossed the Houston area—just to stay busy and to dodge thinking about this gouged hole that widened with every breath and unanswered inquiry of in my body. I was left to care for my Daddy and my brother, by my own promise to my mom.

After postponing my upcoming nuptials for a couple of years, I decided to marry despite my brother's concerns. I found myself in a miserable marriage, lost and confused that my husband had consciously decided to live in the same space, separately.

I felt punished by him and by God, though I knew God did not operate like that. So, I drove to my apartment to stop this torture.

In hindsight, I recognize the enemy's cowardly tactic to attack me while I was suffering from my Momma's death. My grieving, in fact, engulfed my world and became depression.

Overwhelming shame for suicidal contemplations filled my mind so that I was consumed with the enemy's filtered ideas. Feeling alone and lonely, and believing this feeling was everlasting, I had resolved to stop living a lie.

Ironically, no one knew I was suicidal, not my husband (as if the source of my pain cared enough to stop me) and not even my brother. It was a silent and lonely experience with a spirit that was relentless until I began feeding my spirit. Though I prayed, I still suffered in silence.

It was not until God showed me pictures of the two men I loved and admired and vowed to care for—my Daddy and my brother—that I began strengthening my mind and my spirit. "I shall live and not die to declare the works God has planned for me."

Presently, my brother and Daddy are with Jesus, but I know that suicide is not my destiny; it is not God's will for me, or any believer.

Living Her Best LIFE ...or her Best LIE?

So, I know many of you are probably reading this and thinking "Yea ... that's just not me! I love living! I love my life! In fact, I'm living and have lived my best life!" Well you and I, we are the same…

I wasn't necessarily sheltered as a child, but I definitely grew up in the church. I would be in the church 4 out of the 7 longest days of the week. My parents were founding members, so you can only imagine the Baptist upbringing.

I can be pretty rebellious, you know, typical church kid. I experimented with weed and alcohol my freshman year in high school, but couldn't get into it, so I quit. Graduated top 10% of my class, so my parents really didn't harp on me too much when it came to hanging out and partying as long as I took care of business at school and made it home before curfew.

Then I left home for college …. AHHHH! Live a little! I thought? I got involved with an older guy right before leaving for school and that's when things took a turn for the worst. Let's just say this typical A-student never attended class, so she could attend to her cheating boyfriend at his beck and call. Ended up pregnant, had a secret abortion, was asked to get married by him, politely declined.

I had to leave. The situation was toxic.

I really had no idea at the time how that abortion affected me. I went on to live my days as normal and usual like nothing happened really. Until I met this guy, and boy did he make my life feel free! Everything seemed better!

But the two of us, we were dependent on each other and drugs. I steered clear of anything that was highly addictive, though we definitely partied like rock stars. Honestly, I never knew a person could use weed, ecstasy, alcohol, and Xanax (bars) and survive. We were constantly in and out of clubs, college parties, and strip clubs. Endured several late nights and early mornings.

I could go days without eating or sleeping and be perfectly fine. I ended up failing out of school and losing my academic scholarship. Got pregnant again, and miscarried. You see, when you are in a destructive lifestyle, you don't think about the dangers that are around, or the impact of what you are doing, you are just chasing the next high.

I had to move back home with my parents and I was embarrassed by it. I made up lies as to why I was home to save face with a lot of people. I spent the next 6-8 months trying to figure out my life and what to do next.

I took a family vacation for my brother's graduation and he gets murdered right in front of me, and my sisters. Crazy thing is, I was high off of weed, alcohol, and Molly's that night too. I immediately try to conduct CPR on him, just hoping he will survive long enough for the first responders to get there and help.

We make it to the hospital and the doctor comes in and tells us that our brother did not make it. He is "so sorry!" I look to my left and right and its pure chaos. I have a dead brother, a sister trying to strangle herself with a phone cord, another sister running up and down the halls frantic, and my oldest sister having to bear the news to my mother.

The shrill in my mother's voice and the alligator tears from my father are painted so vividly in my mind, nothing could ever hurt me worse.

And me … I was just stuck. In shock I guess. I felt I was to blame. I mean, I started the fight in the club, because I was high. I reflected, "Maybe my CPR was ineffective", because I was high. I questioned God... "Why not me?" My brother was no saint, but he definitely lived better than I did, and he was so young. I mean in hindsight that ideal is suicidal. I thought "Take me instead!"

Took me a long time to get to a place where I stopped using all of it. But my brother's death reminded me the importance of my life. And how I needed to honor him in some way.

This traumatic experience prompted me to remember that life is precious and that I needed to change. So, I did.

And it wasn't easy. Especially when everyone I hang with indulges in the destructive demeanor of smoking, drinking, popping pills, risky sexual encounters, and just wants to party. I definitely suffered from depression and was masking it with the drug use and the partying.

I took a lot of L's: failed relationships, abortions, miscarriages, failed out of school. But no one knew. I mean NO ONE. I was indirectly killing myself, I didn't even realize it. So, I had to separate myself from it and everyone. Including that guy.

I started going back to church and stopped popping pills and smoking weed first. And eventually went back to school. Graduated and went on to get my master's degree. The interesting factor is that multiple people can experience the exact same trauma, at the exact same time, in the exact same place, and cope with it differently.

I took the event and grieved, but allowed it to motivate me to be a better person. My sister however, impulsively, tried to take her own life by strangulation.

I said all that to say this … God Is! I was angry with God for taking my only brother from me. Until I recognized that he is sovereign and makes no mistakes. I questioned God of his power, his love, his purpose, and his plan. I felt my family, especially my parents, didn't deserve this.

My sisters and I joined the Koinonia family and it completely revitalized our relationship with each other. It created a space for us to do life with other believers, and ultimately reignited our relationship with Christ.

You would have no idea that we experienced anything of that magnitude … But GOD!

7
Please … Don't Quit!

Did you have or are you having sex before marriage?

Did you ever have a crush on someone who didn't like you back?

Has anyone ever broken up with you and you didn't understand why?

Were you raised in a one parent home?

Have you ever told a lie and stuck with it?

Have you had more than 3 physical fights?

Have you ever failed at something despite having tried your best?

Have you ever been fired?

Did you grow up in a low-income home?

Have you ever been cheated on or cheated?

Have you ever lost a loved one that you were really close to?

Have you ever been falsely accused?

Have you ever witnessed a woman attacked by a man? (Or Vice versa)

Have you ever been arrested?

Has anyone ever stolen from you? (Or Vice versa)

Is your job stressful?

Have you ever been conned?

Have you ever had an abortion?

Are you raising or have raised a teenager?

These are all issues that can become a breeding ground for depression and/or suicide. Baggage, like the aforementioned, creates a need for personal therapy or counseling from a trained professional. Remember that depression has different forms.

A person can portray themselves as the "life of the party". Consequently, the next morning his or her family member discovers their death by suicide. Many depressed people attend happy hour at local bars, and no one notices the pain behind the glass.

Professional athletes, celebrities, and the famed have thousands of fans cheering their names. Their lives are viewed as perfect and ideal. They are surrounded by entourages but feel alone. This is because the one person that they wish loved them, stares back at them in the mirror and hates the reflection.

You're not crazy! You're a beautiful person who simply needs to open up about what you're going through. The spirit of suicide is like a child predator that swears or threatens its adolescent victim to secrecy.

Moreover, imagine while in the middle of bench pressing a weight you've never tried before, all of a sudden, muscle failure hits. Would you not expect your spotter to assist? Of course, you would!

As a matter of fact, it's unwise to attempt to lift a weight you've never tried before without a spotter in position in case the weight proves to be too heavy. Well guess what. EVERY SINGLE DAY IS a WEIGHT you've never tried to lift before, and I implore by the love of God that you have a spotter in place that you can call on.

As a guy who works out a lot, I've discovered that I never have to ask my spotter for assistance with weight that's too heavy to press. Why? Because a good spotter knows when I'm in trouble before I ask.

Here's the kicker. It does not make me weak when my spotter assists me. I become de facto stronger because I'm now able to lift what was about to crush me. Having a spotter in place makes me bolder to try much heavier weight than I would if I were working out alone! The apostle Paul says it this way,

"For the sake of Christ, then, I am content with weaknesses, insults, hardships, persecutions, and calamities. For when I am weak, then I am strong!"

I believe WHOLEHEARTEDLY that God can heal physically, mentally, and emotionally. I'm a witness that His Grace is most definitely sufficient! I also believe that God oftentimes works through mediums such as doctors, therapists, and counselors.

(Oh, YES I have a therapist! It's been one of the best investments I've ever made in my life.)

Listen, I know what it's like to feel

stuck, like you have no way out. You have to hang in there! I promise that on the other side of this season, greater is coming. Please embrace how much you're loved.

I'm sure I'll never meet everyone who reads this, but despite that, my heart is filled. Tears are in my eyes as I write these concluding words because I love you! I am cheering you on to press forward and not give up!

Don't give up on your family! Don't give up on your friends! Don't give up on yourself! And most importantly, don't give up on God! My prayer is that when things get tough that God holds you close. Please let Him love you.

Believe Him when He whispers that it's going to be ok. He's God. He transcends time and is already in tomorrow waiting on you to get there, so you can start experiencing your best life! Let's end the epidemic here.

Christians DON'T Commit Suicide!

(If you're still wondering what I go to a therapist for in particular...then you most definitely need a therapist.)

Appendix
WARNING SIGNS
AND RISK FACTOR TABLE

Warning Signs	Risk Factors
If a person talks about:	Health Factors
• Killing themselves	• Mental health conditions:
• Feeling hopeless	o Depression
• Having no reason to live	o Substance use problems
• Being a burden to others	o Bipolar disorder
• Feeling trapped	o Schizophrenia
• Unbearable pain	o Personality traits of aggression, mood changes and poor
Behaviors that may signal risk, especially if related to a painful event, loss or change:	

- Increased use of alcohol or drugs

- Looking for a way to end their lives, such as searching online for methods

- Withdrawing from activities

- Isolating from family and friends

- Sleeping too much or too little

- Visiting or calling people to say goodbye

- Giving away prized possessions

relationships

  o Conduct disorder

  o Anxiety disorders

- Serious physical health conditions including pain

- Traumatic brain injury

Environmental Factors

- Access to lethal means including firearms and drugs

- Prolonged stress, such as harassment, bullying, relationship

- Aggression
- Fatigue

People who are considering suicide often display one or more of the following moods:

- Depression
- Anxiety
- Loss of interest
- Irritability
- Humiliation or Shame
- Agitation/Anger
- Relief/Sudden Improvement

problems or unemployment

- Stressful life events, like rejection, divorce, financial crisis, other life transitions or loss
- Exposure to another person's suicide, or to graphic or sensationalized accounts of suicide

Historical Factors

- Previous suicide attempts
- Family history of suicide
- Childhood

	abuse, neglect or trauma

Resources for HELP:

If you or someone you know is in immediate danger:

- o Call 911 or go to your nearest emergency room.

- o If you are in crisis, please call the National Suicide Prevention Lifeline at 1-800-273-TALK (8255) or contact the Crisis Text Line by texting TALK to 741741.

If you or someone you know is battling severe depression or are exhibiting signs:

- o Talk to your Pastor or other church leader

- o Find a local therapist or psychiatrist

You don't have to go through this ALONE!

91656984R00057

Made in the USA
Middletown, DE
06 October 2018